UNITED

...behind the headlines...

Published by the NEWCASTLE CHRONICLE AND JOURNAL LIMITED,
Thomson House, Groat Market, Newcastle upon Tyne, NE1 1ED. (Tel. 0191 2327500)

Contents

The awakening of a sleeping giant

JOHN GIBSON has been reporting on Newcastle United for 30 years and fronted the Evening Chronicle campaign for change which resulted in the Halls coming to power

THE rise of the modern Newcastle United to the very pinnacle of English football is one of the greatest sporting stories ever.

A debt-ridden, once-famous club staring at relegation to the old Third Division, emerged from the ashes of despair to become Premier League runners-up, their highest position for 69 years.

Two men – Sir John Hall and Kevin Keegan – have been the instigators in the rebirth of a club which was more than 100 years old but rapidly becoming a dinosaur.

Keegan had called United "a sleeping giant" but the evidence was that the slumber was more a coma than 40 winks. Yet, in little more than four years, the transformation was complete.

More than £70 million was spent on rejuvenating St. James's Park and the team, as great stars were bought and the club's transfer record smashed time-and-time again.

It had all began with Hall forming the Magpie Group and unleashing a shares war which raged around the corridors of St. James's Park for quite a while. It could never be a bloodless coup and to many it wasn't to be a coup at all.

Hall was given little chance of succeeding by the man in the street but that was to underestimate the courage and the determination to save United not only of Hall, but many faceless loyalists who toiled in his slipstream.

When he did come to power, the real battle was only beginning. Now Sir John and his supporters HAD to deliver just as they had promised. Hollow words or holy deeds?

If there has been a Hallmark of the new regime it's been the ability to surprise with the sheer audacity of some of their decisions. Yet none, perhaps, has surpassed one of their first. Sacking Ossie Ardiles, a respected World Cup winner and defender of the beautiful game,

wasn't too eyebrow-raising in itself – but the appointment of his replacement certainly was!

Since retiring as a player – appropriately with United – Keegan had spent his daylight hours either playing golf at his Spanish home or as a globe-trotting ambassador for football. Eight years had passed without a hint of a sudden lurch in direction.

Then it came . . . Keegan was to be the new manager of Newcastle United! It was sensational in the extreme. Think of KK's credentials. Charismatic, yes. A Tyne folk hero, certainly. A PR dream, definitely. But totally lacking in managerial experience and away from the English game for the best part of a decade.

WHEN Keegan appointed Terry McDermott as his "gofer" it completed the impression of the famous rookies who had a sackful of medals but an empty well when it came to management. "People in football laughed at my appointment and waited for us both to fall flat on our faces," admitted McDermott. Now the only people laughing are United.

In came the stars, up went the fees. Robert Lee, Scott Sellars, Darren Peacock, goalgrabber Andy Cole, the ageless Peter Beardsley, from abroad Philippe Albert and Marc Hottiger, little Ruel Fox. Then, in the summer of last year, the genius of David Ginola, the £4 million talent of Warren Barton, new goal king Les Ferdinand at £6 million, and finally at a staggering £7.5 million Faustino Asprilla from Colombia. Breathtaking landmarks, champion results.

Here we trace the rise and rise of United through the headlines they created and the previously untold inside stories behind those headlines by the men who made them – Kevin Keegan, Terry McDermott, Sir John Hall, vice chairman Freddie Shepherd, director Douglas Hall and chief executive Freddie Fletcher. It's an incredible diary of a meteoric rise.

Edging close to disaster: Ossie's record
of eight wins in 41 league games tells
its own story

Hall verdict on Ossie as Division Three beckons
SAFE AS HOUSES!

2 February, 1992

Douglas Hall . . .

IT'S become one of the most famous quotes around simply because Ossie Ardiles was sacked just days later and the great adventure was under way.

What happened was simple enough. We were playing attacking football but going backwards. Winning friends but losing matches. On this particular Saturday we were away at Oxford United with relegation to the old Third Division on the horizon – unthinkable for a club like Newcastle United.

Freddie Shepherd and I were as usual travelling down by car – Freddie was driving and I was navigating. There was thick fog and when we came to the outskirts of Oxford I got out the road map of the city centre. I was confidently giving instructions to Freddie and, sure enough, we pulled up outside the football ground.

It was deserted and ramshackled. Great, I thought. The only trouble was that we weren't at Oxford United, we were at Oxford City, a non-league ground. A marvellous start!

Anyway, when we eventually got to Oxford United, which was out of town and therefore not on my map, it seemed little better. Robert Maxwell had just left the club and you could see the yellow stains on the walls where the pictures had been taken down!

AS usual, we did all right in the match and lost – 5-2 on this occasion. We were second bottom of the Second Division with the worst defensive record in the league and we knew the Press would be waiting for us. The old vote of confidence seemed a bit hackneyed so I decided to make a joke out of things.

Sure enough, on the way out of the boardroom to the car park I was approached by a reporter asking about Ossie's future and, without breaking stride, I said 'His job's as safe as houses.'

Banner headlines screamed from the newspapers the following day and when we sacked Ossie within a couple of days I got some right stick. Still do, for that matter.

But we couldn't discuss our business in public and I'd thought that if I denied trouble no one would bother quoting me. Well, all I can say is that you know how safe some houses can be these days!

As for Ardiles. He left us with a record of only eight wins in 41 league games which tells its own story I'm afraid.

NEWCASTLE director Douglas Hall last night blasted speculation that manager Ossie Ardiles is facing the axe.

"His job is as safe as houses!" rapped Hall, son of chairman Sir John and a powerful figure in the boardroom in his own right.

And Hall's backing came despite another humiliation as United crashed 5-2 in what was regarded as a make-or-break game at Oxford.

And despite the fact that second-bottom United – with the worst defence in the league – are now staring relegation to

No. 35,716
Wednesday
February 5
1992

22p

Evening Chronicle

LATE
NIGHT
FINAL

OSSIE OUT
KEEGAN IN

Sensation as United move to stop rot

By **JOHN GIBSON**
Sports Editor

NEWCASTLE United produced a double sensation today to rock not only Tyneside but the rest of the country.

United, who are staring relegation to the Third Division in the face for the first time in their history, dramatically sacked manager OSSIE ARDILES.

And they moved swiftly to appoint KEVIN KEEGAN as

5 February, 1992

● FACING THE CAMERAS – Sacked boss Ossie Ardiles is the centre of attention at his Jesmond home

Freddie Shepherd . . .

BRINGING Kevin Keegan in as manager of Newcastle United was the start of it all and one of the most controversial decisions ever made at St James's Park.

It rocked not only Tyneside but the whole of football. And when I look back, the speed of it all was amazing. It was all done and dusted from a standing start to the finish in around 36 hours.

Following the Oxford defeat we knew drastic measures were called for – we couldn't continue to drift or the club would have sunk forever. On the Monday after the game we called a board meeting with Ossie Ardiles to discuss the crisis.

However, he talked about wanting to buy some old players and flog central defender Kevin Scott, who at the time was our prize asset.

Eventually, I took the bull by the horns and asked the 64,000 dollar question: 'Can you keep us up?' Ossie just shrugged his shoulders as only Latins can. That was the moment he signed his death warrant.

If he hadn't faith how the heck could the rest of us – including the fans – have it? If the general's lost it, the troops have no chance.

At the end of the board meeting, Douglas Hall, chief executive Freddie Fletcher and I stayed behind – Sir John was in London at a Conservative dinner dance.

We talked about what to do next and Freddie Fletcher brought up the name of Kevin Keegan. Douglas immediately asked: 'How do you know he'd come?'

Freddie re-assured us – he'd spoken with Kevin Keegan who had told him if ever the Newcastle job came up he'd be interested. That was enough for us.

Douglas Hall . . .

WE flew down to London in a private jet to meet Kevin Keegan – there was Freddie Shepherd, Freddie Fletcher, myself and David Stephenson the former MD of Newcastle Breweries, who was a personal friend of KK from the days when he'd played for us.

Dad was joining us down there. It was all supposed to be hush-hush so you can imagine our distress when we turned up at the Hilton Hotel and found the place swarming with TV cameras. Our first thought was that somehow the news had leaked out – but no, the cameras were there for the showbiz personalities at a Variety Club luncheon. What a relief!

> ## Business is business I'm afraid and the future of Newcastle United was at stake

We were meeting in the privacy of one of the business offices in the hotel – KK had booked and paid for it himself because he knew we were skint.

Dad was a bit perturbed because he'd just had dinner with Ossie that weekend and indicated he'd stand by him. But business is business I'm afraid and the future of Newcastle United was at stake here.

We all went upstairs and within no time at all a deal was done. Kevin was prepared to take over as manager of the club until the end of the season. He wanted Terry McDermott to join him but said he'd pay him himself out of his own pocket – which was more than fair. ! !

5 February, 1992

Freddie Shepherd . . .

FROM London we flew to Southampton so that KK could go home and get some gear. Then it was back to Teesside Airport and on to Sir John's at Wynyard Hall for supper – we had to keep Kevin away from prying eyes. Douglas and I left eventually for the big day ahead.

Handling the changeover was always going to be tricky. We had to break the news to Ossie and to the rest of the board because we'd acted alone. The plan we hatched depended on timing. Ossie would be told at 8 a.m., the rest of the board at 9 a.m. and Kevin would face a Press conference 30 minutes later.

Freddie Fletcher was despatched to Ossie's house while Douglas and I handled the other directors at St. James's Park – in the meantime, Kevin and Sir John headed for the visitors' centre at Newcastle Breweries ready for the Press unveiling.

Ossie was disappointed, of course, but magnificent. He was and has remained an absolute gentleman. Whenever we saw him later at places like Tottenham Hotspur he was most gracious.

The board might have been tricky because at that time we hadn't control of the club – only about 40 per cent of the shares. And we were outnumbered by two to one that morning which meant we could have been outvoted. But they were as stunned as everyone else was to be and that worked in our favour. The board accepted it in silent shock!

A lot of people have said since that we were taking a huge gamble. KK had never managed a football club and had spent most of the eight years since retiring as a player in Spain playing golf. But we knew what we were getting – a winner. We also knew the character of the man. He was a legend!

Douglas Hall . . .

OF course we were gambling – but we weren't betting on a long shot.

We knew that the appointment of Kevin would give everyone a huge lift – our gates doubled immediately.

He lifted the fans. It was a case of the right time, the right man and the right club.

Kevin Keegan . . .

I WOULDN'T have come back into football anywhere else than at Newcastle United. They were a sleeping giant waiting for someone to give them the kiss of life and, remember, I knew all about the fanatical support from when I played here.

Both the club and the team were a shambles and Sir John had made it clear when we met that if we went into the Third Division there mightn't even be a Newcastle United. So I took on the challenge only until the end of the season because it seemed pointless to do anything else.

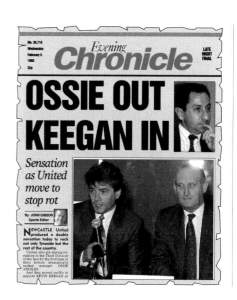

'Kevin
knocked on
the door
and I fell
downstairs
in the dark'

5 February, 1992

'Jean Keegan was on the phone panicking because someone was knocking at her door at 1.30 a.m. – it turned out to be a guy who had a puncture!'

Freddie Fletcher . . .

IT had all been cloak-and-dagger stuff and when we finished at Wynyard Hall the night before the big unveiling, it was late and Sir John and Lady Mae invited me to stay rather than make the trek from Teesside to Newcastle.

I hadn't taken any toiletries with me as I didn't expect an overnight stay so I just clambered into bed. At one thirty in the morning Kevin knocked on my bedroom door – it was pitch dark and being in a strange bedroom I couldn't find the light switch. I staggered to the door in my underpants, opened it, and fell headlong down the stairs. Kevin was in stitches!

It turned out that his wife Jean was on the phone panicking because someone was knocking on the door – they lived in an isolated house and she thought that somehow the story of us appointing Keegan had leaked out and it was the Press wanting interviews. In fact, it turned out to be a guy who had a puncture.

My job the next morning was to inform Ossie

Ardiles that he was sacked. The man was marvellous – he even invited me to have breakfast after I gave him the bad news. His main concern was the whereabouts of the new manager because he wanted to go to the ground, clear out his desk, and say a few goodbyes.

At the time I was living in an hotel and after Ossie left I moved into his club house. The joke goes that while sacking him, I measured the windows for curtains but that's totally untrue of course!

That night back home in Glasgow, my eldest son Alan got on a train with the local newspaper under his arm. He settled down, opened it, and was confronted with the headline: `Axe man's early morning call' with a picture of me underneath. He nearly died.

I suppose it was news up there because previously I'd worked for Glasgow Rangers. That incident probably saw the birth of my nickname Jockweiller but in fact part of my job is to deal with unpleasant decisions. You have to have bottle in this game.

▲ Arab Terry on the day he fooled United over a bid for Kevin Keegan

◀ BACK IN TOWN: Terry McDermott and his wife Carole

It's all happening at St James's
McDERMOTT BACK TO JOIN KEV

7 February, 1992

Terry McDermott . . .

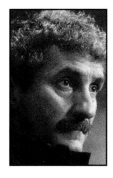

I NEVER expected to come into management when I stopped playing. I'd done very well thank you – won all the honours going with Liverpool – and had a nice pension to fall back on while I enjoyed life. I went into the outside catering business with a pal of mine working at air shows and events like the Grand National.

I used to work out at Anfield just to keep reasonably fit and one day when I returned home David McCreery, who used to play alongside me at Newcastle, phoned to say that Kevin Keegan had got the Newcastle job. I couldn't believe it and put on Teletext to confirm everything.

Kev was an old pal and I didn't think he'd settle for the daily grind but I sent off a congratulations telegram and never thought anything more about it. A few hours later I phoned Mick Quinn at Newcastle – we're both Scousers who liked a bet on the horses and swapped tips. Derek Wright, the physio, answered the phone and told me that KK wanted to speak to me. Still nothing crossed my mind – I said to the missus: 'I wonder what that's all about?' but decided it was just a general chat.

The next day at Anfield, the boot room was full of talk that Kevin was going to offer me a job but he never rang. However, I eventually got the call and Kev was direct as always. He asked if I was willing to help him at St James's Park, stressing that he was staying for only three months to help United escape relegation and wanted me to travel up to the Benwell training ground the next day. It fired my imagination – here was an old mate asking for help at a club where I'd twice been a player and which I loved dearly.

I know a lot of folk might wonder at our partnership seeing us as two very different people. But I thought back to the great times we'd had at Newcastle in the early eighties. We had the same wicked sense of humour – Arthur Cox used to work the players like the SAS so one day KK and I turned up in full army kit crawling through the undergrowth at the training ground. And another time I dressed up in Arab robes, head bowed, and walked into chairman Stan Seymour's office pretending I was making a bid for Keegan.

Kevin Keegan is the most honest man I know in football – he wears his heart on his sleeve and is fiercely loyal as long as you stand shoulder to shoulder. But don't cross him.

If Kevin's appointment had raised a few eyebrows mine sent them through the ceiling. No doubt there were even questioning glances in the boardroom when Kev told them who he wanted to bring in. I know what everyone was thinking: 'What the hell has he done?' But they really didn't know me – and they didn't know Kevin. I'd like to think we've both proved a point since.

Kevin Keegan . . .

TERRY has much more to offer than people think. Of course he has this laugh-a-minute image but, believe me, he's got a very shrewd football brain. Mind you, like me he's got more to offer encouraging the likes of Beardsley and Ginola than we would have if we were trying to get Rochdale or Scarborough out of the Third Division. I knew I was making the right choice four years ago and that assessment hasn't changed.

▲ Sir John Hall flanked by United directors addresses the Press at St James's Park after Keegan's walk-out.

Terry McDermott . . .

THE whole thing will always be remembered for Kevin's famous quote: "It wasn't like it said in the brochure." Well, it wasn't but of course there was an awful lot more to it.

Really the problem was that there was a certain amount of in-fighting on the board at that time and KK was the piggy in the middle. It all became too much – we were both staying at the Gosforth Park Hotel at the time and Kevin decided enough was enough and he was leaving. It was the Friday afternoon before we were due to play Swindon Town on the Saturday and we checked out of the hotel. First we were going south, then we decided on the Lake District. All we wanted to do was get away somewhere totally private and talk.

We got as far as Haydon Bridge when the doubts began to take over. People have said I persuaded the boss to turn the car round and go back but really all he needed was someone to push him. The car was almost turning round on its own!

We thought about the players and the fans and knew we couldn't desert them on the eve of a big game. We never intended to do that. However we still needed to be away from prying eyes and from outside pressures so we decided against going back to the Gosforth Park Hotel and instead booked into Ramside Hall near Durham. It was still Kevin's intention to leave – but not until after the game. We had dinner and sat up just talking and talking in our room.

After breakfast the next morning we motored through to St. James's Park at about 11am just as though nothing had happened. KK didn't transfer any of the pressure on to the players – nothing was said to them. We simply went about the pre-match preparation in exactly the same way as usual. But I must admit it was strange sitting there in the dug-out during the game, watching

KEEGAN WALK-OUT MYSTERY

ST JAMES'S PARK was rife this afternoon with talk that Kevin Keegan had quit as manager of United – and then returned, writes ALAN OLIVER.

But Keegan was still in charge come the kick-off.

Fans huddled together to swap stories that Keegan had checked out of the Gosforth Park Hotel last night with Terry McDermott.

14 March, 1992

▲ RELEGATION SAVIOUR – Keegan spent Hall's money to bring in Brian Kilcline

us win and realising what was going to happen.

On the final whistle Kevin was up and off – he must have been on the A1 before the referee made his dressing-room. I stayed a little longer pottering about during the usual after-game stuff.

By the time I emerged to walk to my car the word had filtered out that something was going on and I was surrounded by the Press. I decided against saying anything and just drove off heading for Liverpool and my family. It was a sad day but I still felt, at such a low moment, that the whole thing could still be rescued. Kevin is a man of principle and had to stick up for what was right but I knew that deep down he wanted to stay. He just needed to hear certain things. If he hadn't made that stand who knows, perhaps everything which has followed would never have happened.

Freddie Fletcher...

THE root of the trouble was that at the time Sir John Hall didn't have complete control and you can't expect someone to put in personal money and have others decide how the club is run. I was aware that Kevin and Terry had left on the Friday but I honestly thought they would return.

Sir John decided to take the other directors down into the Press room after the match and make a public statement. I remember that the windows were open and fans, alerted as to what was happening, were peering in and shouting obscenities. It wasn't pleasant.

I phoned KK in Hampshire on the Sunday. All I could hear was a dog barking madly – that was because a host of reporters were camped at his front door ringing the bell incessantly. While we were talking Kevin's wee girl opened the door and the next thing he knew the reporters were in his living room!

Sir John had also phoned to say that only he and Kevin could save the club. I assured Kevin that John and Lady Mae had lodged a personal cheque at the club for him to spend and eventually he said `Put out a statement and I'll be up on Monday.' That was the cash which bought us Brian Kilcline and Kevin has always said Killer was one of the main reasons we stayed up.

Freddie Shepherd...

KK is a rascal – he's got a great sense of humour. Long after this incident he phoned me at home one morning and announced: "I've been trying to get hold of your mate (Douglas Hall). I'm quitting. I've had enough of this. I'm out."

As you can imagine I was panic stricken. I wasn't certain what had gone wrong but Kevin sounded so convincing. I was halfway down the garden path looking for the cavalry when his final words floated out on the air. "April Fool!"

The Pink

QUINN
ON UNITED
PAGE 13

SAFE!

NEWCASTLE United are safe! They gained a magnificent 2-1 victory at high-flying Leicester in a dramatic finish.

After Gavin Peacock had given United a half-time lead it appeared that victory had been snatched from them at the death when Steve Walsh equalised in the last minute.

But it wasn't all over!

As injury time dragged on Walsh became a villain putting the ball into his own net under pressure from Peacock.

It brought a second pitch invasion from the Leicester fans with the referee taking the players off the field amid confusion about whether or not the game was over.

Eventually, it was announced over the public address system that the match was, in fact, over which meant brave United had secured Second Division football next season by they own efforts without relying on other results.

The decisive breakthrough had come on the stroke of half-time when Peacock beat a possible off-side to crack home his 21st goal of the season and send United fans wild.

But Walsh equalised when he powered in a header which sent the home fans on to the pitch and then scored a shock own goal to wrap up the points for United.

Results back page

■ 2 May, 1992

Kevin Keegan . . .

THE fight against relegation to the old Third Division went right to the wire so when we came to our last home game against Portsmouth it was really win-or-bust stuff. I knew a lot of people turned up hoping to see me buried – well, they were disappointed.

David Kelly scored the only goal of the game late on and our position was absolutely clear cut – if we beat Leicester City at Filbert Street in our final game of the season we would stay up regardless of what others did. And we won 2-1.

But my, was it emotional stuff. They equalised at the death then we won through an own goal with the last kick of the game. I turned to Terry Mac on the touchline and said: 'Tell you what, mate, if they made a film of this people would say it was too far-fetched!' It was a nail-biter, a tremendous achievement. I was off down the tunnel double quick at the end to celebrate.

I said after the match that Newcastle United must never be allowed to go so close to being out of business again. Sir John Hall hadn't control in those days and, with my job done, I just walked away from it. He couldn't give me the financial guarantees I needed to rebuild the club.

Terry and I were like doctors brought in to save a sick patient. Well, the patient was saved and the mission was accomplished.

I knew from day one it would be tough to avoid relegation because by and large the players weren't good enough. I had to bring in some much-needed experience on the cheap – Brian Kilcline, for example, had a major influence on our survival.

■ WISE DECISION: David Elleray

Freddie Shepherd . . .

IT was chaos at Leicester – we won through an injury-time own-goal scored by Steve Walsh and when the ball went in Leicester fans swarmed on to the pitch and the players headed for the tunnel.

For a while, we didn't know if referee David Elleray had abandoned the game or what. We were in limbo, not sure if we were up or down. We were just milling around looking for answers.

But, sensibly, the referee reckoned he'd completed the 90 minutes and we'd won. As it turned out, other results would have kept us up anyway but it was the longest few minutes of my life.

It was always going to be a game of tension – if you remember, Leicester were going for promotion and we were fighting relegation.

We were the best team but they equalised right on the death then the same player – Walsh – put through his own goal to give us a deserved victory. Phew!

Freddie Fletcher . . .

WHEN Leicester City equalised I yelled at Russell Cushing: 'Go and get the other scores. We need to know if we're safe!'

By the time he came back all flustered, I said: 'It doesn't matter, pal. We've won.' The guy could have had a heart attack.

■ CUSHING

Terry McDermott . . .

I REMEMBER driving away from Filbert Street and going past all the Geordies. They were jumping up and down. Honest, it got to me because I knew what it meant to them. My job looked over but I knew we'd given them back their pride.

I know it sounds daft but I felt that moment more than I did when winning the European Cup with Liverpool. That was expected of us but digging out Newcastle over 16 matches was a monumental task.

◀ HOW IT ALL BEGAN – John Hall addresses the Magpie Group at the start of the campaign which catapulted him into power at St James's Park.

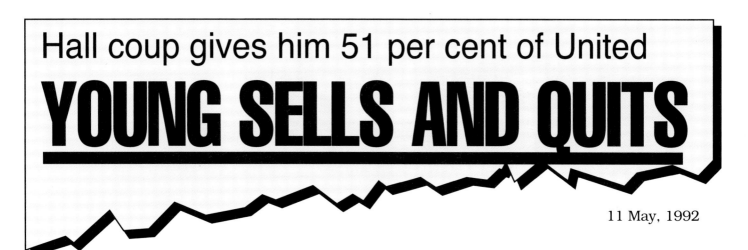

Hall coup gives him 51 per cent of United

YOUNG SELLS AND QUITS

11 May, 1992

Sir John Hall . . .

THE shares fight had been a long and arduous one with a lot of political intrigue. We hadn't had full control when we moved into the boardroom and that stifled a lot of our plans and was the backdrop to Kevin Keegan walking out.

We'd bought out many top shareholders but the significant breakthrough came when we bought director Bob Young's 10 per cent because it meant we owned 51 per cent of the company and were in total charge. We could then move ahead.

There had been many pitfalls along the way – I remember back in November, 1991 I was on a round the world cruise with Lady Mae which was being filmed by Alan Whicker for Whicker's World. I'd decided to retire from my company Cameron Hall Developments at the age of 60.

We owned 40 per cent of Newcastle United and had ploughed in £4 million but at a family meeting decided against topping that up. The public share issue had failed and that was a great disappointment to me because I'd fought the good fight on that platform and didn't want to own a football club. I felt I'd done what I had agreed to do.

Anyway, we were in Hong Kong and were having dinner at a beautiful hotel overlooking a bay when a waiter came over and said: 'You're son has been on the phone.

Could you give him a ring?' I was intrigued.

It turned out that the other directors had called in Douglas

▶ BOB YOUNG

and Freddie Shepherd to say that the club was in danger of going to the wall. They wanted a public rights issue to raise more capital but warned that if we didn't take up our 40 per cent Newcastle United would fold.

I was in the middle of a holiday on the other side of the world and asked Douglas if the whole thing couldn't be put on ice for two weeks until I returned. His reply was stark and to the point: 'You've got two hours to decide, dad, not two weeks!'

Douglas convinced me that we couldn't let a great institution like the football club die and that we must save it. That phone call cost me £680,000 and saved Newcastle from bankruptcy. It was a tale not told on Whicker's World and it was one of many crises we encountered along the way to full control.

▲ ALAN WHICKER

21 May, 1992

▲ BACK IN CHARGE – Kevin Keegan back at St James's Park after a United delegation flew out to Spain for talks.

Douglas Hall . . .

HAVING completed the job of keeping us up Kevin Keegan had shot off to his house in Marbella, Spain. The summer weeks were beginning to pass with plenty of speculation on Tyneside as to who would be Newcastle's manager when the new season kicked-off.

It was decision time and we decided to fly out to Spain to see Kevin and thrash things out. I went with the two Freddies – Shepherd and Fletcher.

We met KK in an hotel with Jean and the kids relaxing on the other side of the swimming pool.

Freddie Shepherd . . .

WHAT Keegan wanted to see was our business plan and some clarification of the Halls' position so he knew who he was working for. We satisfied him on both counts and agreed a three-year contract with Terry Mac appointed as his assistant – and we would pay his wages this time!

While we were nattering we mentioned the name of Chris Waddle and asked if Kevin fancied signing him. "Sure," he said, so off we flew to Marseille on the second leg of our European jaunt. We met Chris at his house in Aix en Provence and he was more than interested. It actually never happened for a variety of reasons – he was keen to get on to the coaching side as well as playing – but it was a highly successful trip because bringing Keegan back was the key to everything that has happened since then.

Kevin Keegan . . .

IT was a totally different ball game when I agreed to go back to St James's Park – I was able to manage the club the way I wanted to.

A lot of people in football hadn't liked it when a bloke who had been out of the game for eight years got a job like the one at Newcastle United and then appointed another outsider in the shape of Terry McDermott. They wondered why we got the opportunity when they'd been around all the time.

Well, we'd proved ourselves and we each got a three-year contract. If I'd asked for Terry Mac to be put on such a contract right from the start the board would probably have knocked me back. But I knew he loved the club and was very loyal, which was essential. He came, did his stuff alongside me as my consultant paid by me, and now we were in business.

Terry McDermott. . .

AT one stage I was resigned to the fact that we weren't returning to United. If there was no Kevin Keegan there was no Terry Mac – I would return to life in the quiet lane. Then one day I received a phone call out of the blue from Kevin who said: 'We're going back, pal.' That was enough – I packed my bags and moved the family up North.

◀ CHRIS WADDLE – also in talks with United

◀ FAMILY AFFAIR – Robert Lee and son Oliver soak up the St James's Park atmosphere after his £700,000 move from Charlton

▶ UNITED: In comes hot-shot winger

UNITED SET TO GET LEE

22 September, 1992

Kevin Keegan . . .

WE had a bit of fun over this transfer – Robert Lee had turned down Middlesbrough because it was too far away from London and then I convinced him that Newcastle was closer!

Actually that's not as daft as it sounds. Tyneside IS closer if you're talking about commuting.

I pointed out that if he'd wanted to go home from Middlesbrough he would have to get a taxi to Darlington Station and even then, a lot of fast trains from Newcastle to Kings Cross don't stop there. And if he wanted to fly there were about two flights a day from Teesside but half a dozen from Newcastle.

I also pointed out that United were a much bigger outfit than Boro in virtually every way. I didn't want to be unkind but it was a fact.

Robert was a player who had stayed at one club, Charlton Athletic, all his life. He'd lived in the same street and had the same friends – it was time to broaden out. A whole new world opened up to him here and to be fair, he has grown with it.

I originally saw him as a player to work the right wing as he was strong and had something to prove. I saw him as very similar to Steve Stone at Forest – he could beat people, score goals and track back to help in defence.

But as he developed, I wanted to use him where he could influence a game more that's why I moved him into midfield.

I've said he's the best midfielder in England and I mean that. Of all my signings – and there's been some good 'uns – I have to pick out Robert Lee at just £700,000.

And he's gone on raising his standards in line with the way we've raised Newcastle United's standards.

◀ BRAVE NEW WORLD – Robert Lee broadened his horizons when he signed for United where Kevin Keegan compared him with Gateshead-born Steve Stone (far left)

▶ Newcastle make it 11 wins out of 11

CLASS HAS FINAL SAY

IT took a stunning strike from that Irish stroller Liam O'Brien to win the 115th derby.

But in reality, the class side was streets ahead in ability. Newcastle United deserved to make it 11 wins out of 11 because they were the true technicians.

18 October, 1992

SUNDERLAND 1 NEWCASTLE UNITED 2

Kevin Keegan . . .

WE were quick out of the blocks that season rattling up 11 consecutive wins culminating with a great derby victory for the fans at Roker Park to prove we could win matches playing good football.

But to be truthful, I remember the game after Sunderland much more – we'd seemingly done the hard bit, came home to play Grimsby and lost! I can see their fella scoring the goal to this day.

If we'd won that game we could have gone on to set real records. It proved what football can do to you – just when you consider you've got it right up pops the devil!

Douglas Hall . . .

Jubilation as Liam O'Brien scores United's winner direct from a free-kick and ▼ sets off on a celebration run

I'VE got two photographs framed and hung in my snooker room at home – one is of Liam O'Brien's winning goal at Roker Park and the other of Scott Sellars' goal in the return at St. James's Park.

That game was played with puddles all over the pitch after torrential rain – we'd borrowed big sponges to make certain the game would be played.

I was flying out of Newcastle Airport at 7.0 pm after the Roker match and straight after O'Brien's superb free-kick I had to dash out to my car.

I was driving through Sunderland town centre with the radio blaring and the window wound down. On the final whistle I was so overjoyed I gave a clenched fist salute.

I guess I would have been lynched if the locals could have got at me.

The travelling fans that season were unbelievable – I remember an earlier match at Peterborough in our winning start. We went down by train which was packed to the rafters.

The Toon Army wouldn't allow swearing because mam was there and they literally carried mam and dad shoulder high across the main road, stopping all the cars. It was quite a sight.

◄ SEAT OF POWER – Chairman Sir John Hall with President Trevor Bennett

Freddie Fletcher . . .

TREVOR BENNETT is perhaps a name not too familiar with our supporters who think about the Halls and Freddie Shepherd when it comes to the board of directors but he was a very important acquisition at a time when we were re-structuring the financial side of a club £6 million in debt. Trevor's input, not just financially, in the rise of Newcastle United has been invaluable even if the public don't fully realise it. Key signings aren't confined to the field of play of course.

I'd been here about eight months when I became aware that a Trevor Bennett had given the club a £500,000 interest free loan. I asked Russell Cushing: "Who is he? What's the story?" It transpired that Trevor had been brought to games by a former director Peter Mallinger, who also lived in Leicester, so I phoned Trevor asking if he would attend a meeting with myself and Freddie Shepherd at St. James's.

Freddie Shepherd

AT that meeting we thanked Mr Bennett for his help, outlined our ambitious plans for the future, and asked: "Would you like to come into the fold?"

Because he was impressed with the jobs being done by the Halls and Kevin Keegan he not only agreed but made another half million pounds available if required. Eventually Trevor gave us two other loans of £500,000 – the shortfall on the Andy Cole transfer and another boost as we progressed. He became an associated director, then president and finally a full director, which is his current position.

PRESIDENT BENNETT GIVES UNITED £1m

8 March, 1993

Sir John Hall . . .

TREVOR BENNETT was there when United needed him most. And he has been supportive to the tune of £2 million. Our signing of Andy Cole couldn't have been completed without him and we know what exciting times that deal heralded. It took one phone call from Douglas about Cole and the money was immediately made available to the club.

Trevor Bennett .

I'VE always been sports minded – I was the major shareholder at Leicester City and have been involved with Leicestershire County Cricket Club for some time. They kindly named the section where their indoor school is housed 'The Bennett End' and made me their first Life President after I helped them out.

What I liked about the Newcastle United set-up from the start is that the people who now run the club are incredibly tough – amazingly tough even with each other. They fight like fury all the time so as not to take a single step backwards in their pursuit of perfection.

They each have their own inimitable style and authority and the constant way they are so clear minded and lucid under pressure never ceases to amaze me. I knew my £2 million was in safe hands. They will never be surpassed in football.

My years with Newcastle United have unquestionably been my happiest in sport. And not just because of what has been achieved but by what will be achieved.

▶ "Our signing of Andy Cole couldn't have been completed without Trevor Bennett" – Sir John

● COMING CLEAN: Andy Cole moved to Newcastle United to put the opposition defences in a spin

Douglas Hall . . .

WE'D tried to sign Andy Cole several times each time putting in a higher bid but Bristol City would have none of it because they had a sell-on clause which meant that his old club Arsenal got a big slice of the fee.

Then one day, we were having lunch at a restaurant in Jesmond and Kevin Keegan joined us. Dad was talking about how important it was for Newcastle to win the First Division championship and get into the Premiership.

He turned to Kevin and said: 'Is there anything we can do?' Back came the answer: 'Get me Andy Cole.' That was it – we were off to St. James's and dad instructed Freddie Fletcher to phone Bristol City.

They have about 13 people on their committee and amazingly they were meeting that very after-noon. It was too good an opportunity to miss so we smacked in a £1.7 million bid. Trevor Bennett, our president, helped, our shirt sponsors Asics helped, and we put in some dough ourselves – we were mortgaged up to the hilt.

But we'd had enough of waiting and told them if they didn't come back with an answer in five minutes we'd be off and spend our money elsewhere. Sure enough, they were back on the phone accepting the bid.

That's when the trouble started. We asked City to get Cole to phone KK but they didn't know where he was. Eventually they found his car parked in town and left a note on his window saying 'please contact the chairman.' Andy, a bachelor, was actually doing his clothes at a nearby laundry!

► Newcastle smash transfer record for England Under-21 striker

£1.7m SIGNING

Cole snapped up – 12 March, 1993

Kevin Keegan . . .

A LOT of people in the game were negative about Andy Cole. He'd been allowed to leave Arsenal and some said it was because he had an attitude problem.

But the kid was only 21 and Terry MacDermott and I liked the look of him. We felt that if we worked on him and got him the right partner he could become something really special.

"Well, he was just that, wasn't he? In our First Division championship season Cole scored a dozen goals in 11 starts and went on to bag a staggering 41 goals in our first Premiership season. He's in the record books forever."

I'd first thought of Andy when I saw him out-run Steve Howey on the touchline by running off the pitch and then coming back on. One night shortly before 5 p.m. I was sitting in the club offices at St James's Park with Terry Mac when we saw that Bristol City were playing West Ham that night with a 7.45 kick-off.

We were just saying how geography was against Newcastle – if we'd been further south we could have gone to the game to watch Cole – when Douglas Hall popped his head round the door.

The next moment we were on Cameron Hall's private jet heading for Bristol. Andy was playing despite an injury and I liked that. It showed he had guts and wouldn't always be looking to come off. He was sensational so when we had a lunch to celebrate the sponsorship deal with Asics I thought: 'Why don't we spend some of the cash?'

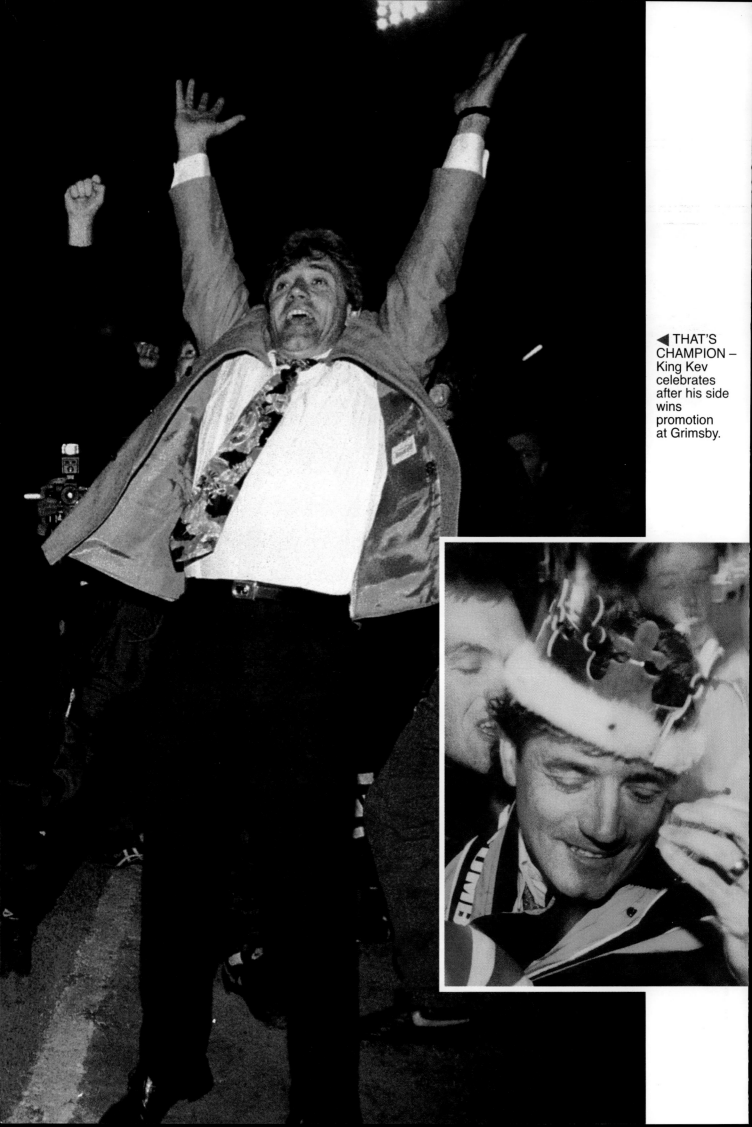

◀ THAT'S CHAMPION – King Kev celebrates after his side wins promotion at Grimsby.

WE'RE ON OUR WAY

NEWCASTLE United chairman Sir John Hall today hailed the First Division championship as "our glorious achievement" and proudly forecast promotion to the Premier League is only the beginning.

Sir John was at Grimsby last night to see the team he gave manager Kevin Keegan £6m to build clinch the ultimate prize to spark off a huge celebration

4 May, 1993

GRIMSBY 0 NEWCASTLE 2

Kevin Keegan . . .

IT was a great night, the culmination of all our work. But it was a pity it wasn't at St. James's Park in front of our own fans but to be truthful, there were so many Geordies at Grimsby the atmosphere was extra special.

At the end of the game, our fans were all over the place and someone stuck a crown on my head and the photographers grabbed the picture. Where on earth the guy got it from I'll never know.

Freddie Shepherd . . .

THE Grimsby directors were fantastic. I remember going into the boardroom and there was a mountain of fish fingers on a silver platter – and I mean a mountain. They could have fed the whole of Tyneside. Evidently, they had

a sponsorship deal with the frozen food firm Findus. After our victory John Hall and I walked across the pitch to get to the dressing-rooms on the opposite side and the whole place was a sea of black and white. When we got back to the boardroom the Grimsby directors already had the champagne open for us to celebrate. A thoughtful touch, wasn't it?

Douglas Hall . . .

I WAS in Athens on business and getting the scores on my mobile phone. There'd been a delay after our second goal and it seemed the game would never end. I sank a few drinks that night, I can tell you.

Sir John . . .

LADY MAE and I travelled to the game by car and stopped off at a Little Chef on the M62 for a coffee. We'd paid the bill and were just leaving when a transit van pulled up in the corner of the car park and a load of Newcastle supporters climbed out. How they'd all managed to squeeze into the van I'll never know.

With their backs to us they all began relieving themselves. I shouted: 'Right, you lot. Let me have your season tickets. You're banned.' They looked around with startled expressions on their faces and shot back into the van without doing themselves up!

I managed to keep a straight face, delivered a lecture to them about letting Newcastle United and Geordies down, and off they went all sheepish. I guess they really celebrated later on.

Premier class United

No one could have lived with us that day

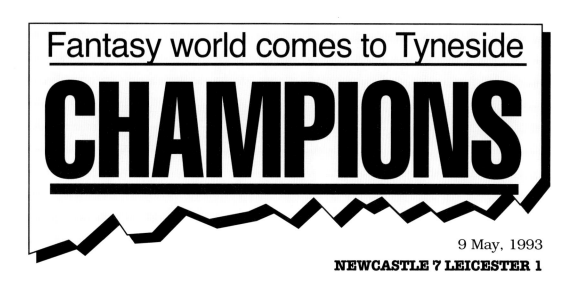

Fantasy world comes to Tyneside

CHAMPIONS

9 May, 1993

NEWCASTLE 7 LEICESTER 1

Kevin Keegan . . .

NO one would have lived with us that day. As a one-off game it was as perfect as I could have wished – 7-1 is some way to round off a championship season, isn't it? And remember Leicester were no slouches. They made the play-off finals at Wembley that season. It was ironic that exactly a year after we had to win at Leicester on the last day to avoid the Third Division we should beat the same side to be champions.

With a couple of minutes to go to half-time I stood with Terry Mac looking round the ground. We were six goals ahead and the whole place was a sea of black and white. You couldn't hear yourself speak for the din. We just drank in the atmosphere.

I wanted the boys to have a party. We could have lost 1-0 or 2-1 and the fans would probably have accepted it because we were up but I was desperate to finish with a flourish. I wanted to let the Premier League know we were coming – to put a shot across their bows.

FOOTBALL League champions Newcastle United are today the toast of Tyneside.

United's delirious fans are in seventh heaven after a record-smashing 7-1 victory over shell-shocked Leicester City brought the St James's Park celebration party to a perfect ending yesterday.

United amassed 96 points and 29 victories to lift two championship trophies on an occasion chairman Sir John Hall described as "the party to end all parties – the day we were all proud of OUR club."

Six extra-ordinary goals in the first-half brought tears of joy to the faces of fans brought up on a starvation diet of success over the years since the early fifties.

Sir John Hall . . .

Douglas Hall . . .

I'VE only got three United videos at home – this victory, the 3-0 win over Liverpool when Andy Cole wrecked them in the first-half and the 5-1 slaughter of Brentford in our promotion season when Robert Lee scored the best goal of the match from inside our own half and it was chalked off!

What a way to finish our championship season – a memory to cherish. It was a real party atmosphere, we

even had Lindisfarne giving a pop concert before the match. Fog on the Tyne? We blew that away, all right.

IT was 6-0 at half-time, the most breathtaking 45 minutes ever. I was so elated that I was walking from private box to private box with a bottle in my hand pouring everyone a drink. I even went up onto the television gantry and sang a song to the crew – I don't think they were too impressed by my voice!

You're in football for days like this. I reckon everyone in the ground was standing up singing the Andy Cole song. This is what Newcastle United are all about.

Douglas Hall . . .

WE had a parade through the city from the Gosforth Park Hotel down to the Civic Centre with the First Division championship trophy and I remember wearing a neck brace because I'd damaged my shoulder.

I had a black and white rosette pinned on it – I must have looked a right pillock. I remember the coach nosing its way through Gosforth and I saw Tessa McKeag, wife of the former Newcastle United chairman Gordon McKeag, watching and waving. I thought that was nice in view of the shares war which had just been fought.

As we approached the Civic Centre a small boy was trying desperately to get some autographs from the players. We pulled him aboard the bus and said: 'Now get them yourself!' He was dumbstruck.

KK hadn't wanted to be on the celebration ride – he wanted to leave the glory to the players. But we knew the part he'd played and persuaded him he must be there. It wouldn't have been the same for the fans without Kevin Keegan.

▲ HAT-TRICK HEROES – Andy Cole and David Kelly celebrate the seven-goal rout.

▼ TOAST OF TYNESIDE – Keegan and the United team salute the Toon Army

▲ PASS MASTER – Peter Beardsley pictured with his old games master from Longbenton High School, Jim Giles, on the day the England international returned to St James's Park

I'LL FINISH THE JOB

— says new boy Beardsley

8 July, 1993

Kevin Keegan . . .

THIS was a very special deal – I was actually due to sign Peter and the Russian striker Sergei Yuran on the same day. Yuran, you may remember, played for Benfica and Porto and ended up on-loan at Millwall. Everton had turned me down at first and ironically Arthur Cox was trying to get Beardsley for Derby County at the same time as we were in for him.

I was due to meet Peter at an hotel in Wetherby but when I got there with Terry Mac, the board were still haggling about his age. I'd actually made a rod for my own back when I signed Andy Cole by going on about how young he was and therefore what an investment he would be. Then I went out and tried to sign a player the wrong side of 30! I could understand the apprehension but then they didn't know Peter Beardsley like I did.

I saw Peter and his agent Des Bremner walking across the car park into the hotel but I was still arguing my case on the car phone and told Terry to drive round the block while I continued to put my point of view.

I was speaking with Freddie Shepherd, who was relaying the board's feelings over the phone, and he told me to sign Yuran first and then Beardsley so that the average age of the team went down. They wanted the security of at least having Yuran as well as Peter but I explained that I wasn't due to see the Russian until 4 p.m. and that if I drove away from Wetherby I'd lose Beardsley. I thought 'to heck with it' so I told a fib and said that Sunderland were in for Peter and they would get him if we didn't. 'Sign him,' said Freddie Shep immediately, so in we went.

I knew what I was doing. I knew we were buy-

PETER Beardsley breezed back to Tyneside today and rejoined Newcastle United on a three-year contract.

By ALAN OLIVER

And the 32-year-old former United favourite said: "It's great to be back to help the club finish off the job the boss started nine years ago."

Speaking at a Press conference before going through the formalities of his medical, Beardsley, who will cost United £1.3m in his move from Everton, said: "Everything about this club last season was magnificent and I don't see why things should be any different this time around.

"I saw them play a couple of times last season including the home game with Luton and I don't think, while there was one or two disappointments, they had a bad game.

"I always wanted to come back but I wasn't sure that I would be given the chance. I thought my last move

ing Premiership credibility. No one could be sure that Andy Cole, John Beresford or Robert Lee could play in the top flight because they hadn't done it, but with Peter there was no such risk. And he was willing to take a drop in wages to come!

After sorting out Beardsley we shot up to Teesside in the car and caught a plane to Heathrow where we met Yuran and a host of agents speaking Portuguese and Italian. We didn't like the questions asked so we ended up buying Beardsley and not Yuran which was the wrong way round for the board. But they deserve credit for the way they took it.

● SERGEI YURAN

I'LL FINISH THE JOB
— says new boy Beardsley

8 July, 1993

◄ "What Beardsley has done for Newcastle is monumental" – Sir John

Freddie Shepherd . . .

DOUGLAS HALL and I were at a wedding in Nottingham when we were eventually tracked down at our hotel by KK.

He said: 'Where have you been? I'm sitting outside a hotel with Terry McDermott – Peter Beardsley's inside and I want to know if we can speak to him.'

He later tried the old Sunderland trick with Tino Asprilla as well – but it didn't work that time.

Sir John Hall . . .

I KNEW what a quality player Beardsley was, of course, but I'm a business man and my job is to protect Newcastle United. I was worried about signing for £1.3 million a player who was over 30 and would have no sell-on value at the end of his contract.

I was in Spain when Douglas phoned me about the deal and he told me that Peter was 32 – but I happened to have a football Who's Who, I looked him up, and found he was actually 33. I'd complained when United had bought Roy Aitken because I thought he was too old and here we were doing it again.

However, they persuaded me that we should still do it and I'm glad they did. I was wrong – what Beardsley has done for Newcastle is monumental. Why, even England recognised that recalling him to the international team after a three-year absence. However, he is the exception rather than the rule.

£2.7m PEACOCK

Darren signs after £7m double bid to land Ferdie fails

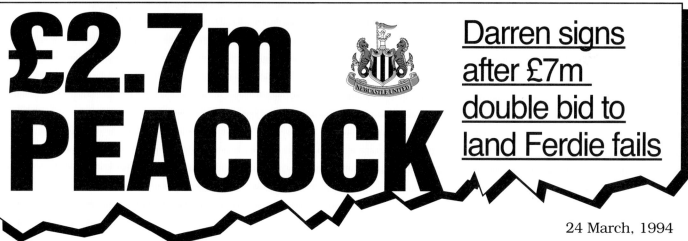

24 March, 1994

Kevin Keegan . . .

WE paid what was then a club record fee of £2.7 million for Darren Peacock at a time when we were also interested in Les Ferdinand at QPR. I watched Peacock personally five times and asked Andy Cole: "Who are the best three defenders you've played against?" One of them was Darren which spoke volumes.

He flew up north after we'd beaten Ipswich Town 2-0 and I went to see him. It took half an hour to agree terms!

KEVIN Keegan today again broke Newcastle United's record transfer fee when he paid QPR £2.7m for their 26-year-old Darren Peacock.

And I can exclusively reveal that United tried to make it an amazing £7m double swoop by signing Peacock's teammate Les

Douglas Hall . . .

OUR original bid was £2.2 million but Rangers held out for an extra half a million pounds. Dad and mam had to finance the transfer with a loan because the bank money was being used on the ground.

This was another case of a knock-on effect in transfers – in fact our dough saved Third Division Hereford United because they had a 10 per cent sell-on clause with QPR. Actually, the £260,000 they received as part of our deal was bigger than the original fee they got for Peacock which was £200,000.

When Rangers eventually sold Ferdie to us it was non-league Hayes who copped the extra cash. Aye, small clubs love us!

▲ Together after more than a decade apart – Kevin Keegan introduces Arthur Cox at a press conference which also marked the United manager signing a 10-year contract.

▶ Together for the first time – manager Arthur Cox shows off his star signing Kevin Keegan at a press conference back in 1982

10 YEARS Incredible new deal for Keegan

4 May, 1994

Douglas Hall . . .

WE were the bold guys who brought Kevin Keegan back into football and we weren't about to let someone else nick him. England were sniffing and we had to be positive. We knew that a 10-year contract is extremely unusual for a football manager but that didn't bother us. We knew KK was the right man when we went for him originally and nothing had changed. We wanted continuity – that's the way you get success.

We were asking our fans at the time to join a bond scheme and felt that we couldn't ask them for a long term commitment if we didn't show the same dedication with our management team. It was our idea to offer Kevin a 10-year deal and the title director of football but he was delighted when approached. There was no question where he wanted his future to be.

Arthur Cox . . .

KEVIN came down to Derby to see me when I was suffering from a prolapsed disc – I had quit as manager at the Baseball Ground because of my condition. Kevin was laughing and joking when he came through the front door, but when he saw me, he was shocked at my condition.

We had always kept in touch since I was manager here and he came another three or four times that year. In between those visits we kept in touch by phone. For my part I watched Newcastle a few times on telly and it was good to see them winning in such style. I knew how much that would mean to the supporters on Tyneside.

Then in the April Kevin invited me to the game against Liverpool at Anfield. It was such an emotional day what with Kevin and Terry McDermott going back there as well as Peter Beardsley and Barry Venison. And, of course, it was the fifth anniversary of the Hillsborough tragedy – it was really a special Saturday afternoon to be involved with Newcastle and what capped it was the way the team played. The 2-0 scoreline flattered Liverpool.

The next thing I knew, Kevin asked me to join him full-time and I was back where I belong.

Kevin Keegan . . .

THE job felt right and I wanted to see it through. I wanted players to know when I talked terms with them that I was totally committed to the rebuilding of the club.

At the same Press conference when my new contract was announced we also announced that Arthur Cox had returned to the club. Arthur was the man who signed me for Newcastle as a player back in the early 80s and I liked his integrity, loyalty and football knowledge. To me he was our Bill Shankly – and people know what I thought about Shanks!

▶ PHILIPPE ALBERT

IT'S GREAT TO BE HERE!

10 August, 1994

Terry McDermott . . .

WE were first alerted about Philippe Albert when we were playing in the Glasgow pre-season tournament. I took a phone call on my mobile in the grounds of our hotel and it was from an agent who had five days to sell Albert to an English club.

I know for a fact that he also approached Liverpool, who were quite interested, and I believe Blackburn Rovers were also contacted.

The gaffer had spent the summer out in America doing TV work on the World Cup finals and he knew all about Philippe who had starred for Belgium. He rated him highly and fancied a dabble straight away. Kevin always makes up his mind quickly about someone – I remember once when we went up to Scotland to watch a player and he turned to me as the guy ran out the tunnel and said: "He's no good to us." The fella hadn't even kicked a ball! It was all to do with his shape and the way he moved. What's more, Kevin was right – he wasn't worth signing.

Anyway, within three days we were meeting Albert at Leeds-Bradford Airport. He had a Geordie mate, Peter Harrison, with him – they had played together as the two centre-halves at Charleroi in Belgium at the beginning of Philippe's career. Which didn't do us any harm because having a Geordie and a pal on our side was a good start.

We went to an hotel, laid on sandwiches and orange squash, and within two hours the deal was done. Albert was up in the Gosforth Park Hotel that night.

Kevin Keegan . . .

PHILIPPE ALBERT is a world class player – bringing him and David Ginola to this club gave me a real buzz. It's more difficult for foreign players to settle in but Philippe was at home from day one.

He gave us a different dimension and the character of the man was shown by the way he battled back from that horrific training injury which kept him out for a year. The man has the ability to defend, pass, and score goals.

● CLASS ACT – £2.65 million central defender Philippe Albert signs for United

▲ SHAKE ON IT –
Scott Sellars and
Andy Cole celebrate
United's fifth goal at
St James's Park.

▶ SHIRT
SWAPPERS –
Philippe Albert, a
Belgian
international of
course, salutes the
crowd in an
Antwerp shirt while
◀ Kevin Keegan
gives a hug to one
of the Belgians after
the first leg match

ROYAL ANTWERP 0 NEWCASTLE UNITED 5

C'est magnifique

13 September, 1994

Terry McDermott . . .

OUR first season in the Premier League had seen us finish third top and qualify for the UEFA Cup which was quite an achievement. Since my first manager at United, Joe Harvey, had won the old European Fairs Cup in 1969 and spent a few seasons in Europe the club had only played in the competition once during the fleeting reign of Richard Dinnis almost 20 years ago. So it was a bit special for Tyneside.

And didn't we march back on to the Continent in style? Our first match was away to Royal Antwerp and we massacred them 5-0 to raise eyebrows throughout the country.

It was as good as the scoreline suggests, too – I won three European Cups with Liverpool so I know what I'm talking about and, take it from me, this was as good a one-off performance as I've seen in European football. Sure, Liverpool played in bigger matches but as a single game this was a show which rocked a lot of people. Antwerp weren't a bad side but there was no way they were going to compete with us on the night.

Rob Lee scored a hat-trick of headers and that alone underlines our domination. Headers? Rob? We could have done anything in that game.

Think about it – we were one up after only 50 sec-onds, two up in eight minutes and three up by half-time. That's taking Europe by the scruff of the neck.

Freddie Fletcher . . .

WHILE everything went right on the park in Antwerp it was a shambles off it – so much so that we lodged a formal complaint to UEFA. We stayed strictly within their guidelines on our return to Europe, got a slagging from our fans because of it, and then found that Royal Antwerp were ignoring all the rules.

UEFA insist that supporters are taken in and out of the city on the day of the match with no overnight stays – obviously for safety reasons – and we organised our packages to abide within the rules. We were even told not to give out match tickets until we were en route to prevent fans from travelling early. I didn't like it but I understood their thinking. Our supporters, however, were extremely unhappy because they naturally wanted to see something of the place and we were accused of trying to make financial gain.

Imagine our horror, then, when we discovered that Antwerp were selling tickets openly to United fans without segregation and well in advance of the match. We immediately lodged an official complaint to UEFA in case there was trouble but got absolutely nowhere.

Then when we saw the stadium our fears increased. It was like a building site, full of bricks and rubble. I walked round it and pulled a huge piece of iron out of the ground with one hand. A thug could have used it to whack an opposing fan over the head. Again we lodged a formal complaint at the morning meeting with UEFA and to be fair this time they ordered a clean up of the stadium. But still parts of it collapsed during the match – we had our own police observers and stewards there and they were appalled.

Frankly, we have learned from our experiences and next season we will allow any season ticket holder to buy tickets for our games abroad and make their own way there. Our fans have earned the right to be treated well and we'll inform UEFA of our stand.

Kevin Keegan . . .

WE showed that you can go into Europe and play exciting, attacking football without travelling with fear. Our style was not to defend in an away leg. It was extremely satisfying without the naivety we showed at home in the next round.

Not only did we make people sit up and take notice in Belgium but we won through by scoring 10 goals and swamping Antwerp 5-2 in the return leg at St. James's.

Even the great teams of the past would have been proud of such a demolition job.

◀ FOX AND HOUNDS – Ruel Fox is buried by the pack after his ninth-minute goal had given the Magpies a super start at St James's Park.

► NEWCASTLE 3 ATHLETICO BILBAO 2

YOU'RE WARNED

18 October, 1994

Terry McDermott . . .

OH, no. I can still see it now – 3-0 up at St. James's after less than an hour and apparently coasting. Then the Mexican Wave starts on the terraces, it's carnival time, and we concede two goals in the last 20 minutes. That's when the tie was lost.

We were naive all right. The crowd thought it was all over after Fox, Beardsley and Cole scored and so did the players. But KK and I have won the European Cup and we knew differently. We could sense the atmosphere wasn't condusive to keeping a clean sheet and when Bilbao got their first we were angry. The crowd weren't bothered – it was still 3-1 – but we knew on the bench that it was bad crack with the away goal rule. Then, crickey, they got a second and could easily have made it 3-3.

Looking back, it was a learning process for the players. They paid the greatest price and they won't do it again. The Mexican Wave didn't help, of course, but the players should have been professional enough to have coped.

Freddie Shepherd . . .

THE Bilbao directors, thinking we'd be pleased about their links with the North East of England, regaled us with tales about how a guy from the Sunderland shipyards had gone over and formed their club which is why they played in red and white stripes. Which was terrific when we lost of course! However, the truth was that we formed a great friendship between the two clubs and two sets of fans.

▲ AGONY – Steve Howey can't believe it as United go out in Bilbao on the away goals rule

The Palace of

St James's Park

► UNITED MOVE INTO THE 21st CENTURY

GROUNDS FOR PRIDE

Russell Jones . . .

Managing director of Cameron Hall Developments Ltd and the Newcastle
United director who masterminded the rebuilding of St. James's Park

IT was a unique challenge to re-develop St. James's Park because this was a living stadium in a city centre. We couldn't close it down to work on it, as you can with other projects, and we weren't starting from scratch but building on to a standing structure.

We didn't want to create the usual run-of-the-mill designs but make a statement that we were the best. We wanted to create a major landmark in the city and a tourist attraction and I believe we've achieved that.

The difficulty was to make St. James's look like one complete stadium and not a ground where bits had merely been built on to it. We ended up spending £25 million on St. James's which is a huge amount – you can build a completely new ground for less. However, there was a price to pay for keeping the place open throughout all the alterations – we had to keep bums on seats yet still create a ground which matched our development on the field. Both had to go hand in hand. It was like putting on a West End show every other week but still working on the stage at the same time.

First we had to get the approval of the city council and the freemen and overcome the

◄ St James's Park after redevelopment in 1905 with the new West Stand seating 4,680 spectators. The stadium remained like this into the 1930s.

► St James's, with both ends behind the goals open, before the Hall redevelopment.

inevitable protestors. Then we had to start the jigsaw piece-by-piece – the old Leazes End becoming the Sir John Hall Stand, extend the roof of the Milburn Stand, create the Gallowgate End and, at the same time, completely relay the pitch.

The closing of Strawberry Place was the key – if we had been unable to do that we would have had to lay out the material on the pitch itself which would have prevented us putting in the sprinkler system, the drainage, and returfing at the same time.

Oh, it became hairy all right! The clock was always our enemy – I remember battling desperately to get the ground ready for the opening match of the 1993-94 season against Spurs.

The workmen toiled 24 hours a day seven days a week. We even turned on the floodlights so that they could operate throughout the night. I think it was the goodwill Newcastle United create which made it all possible – the workmen were virtually all supporters and the suppliers and sub-contractors, etc. nearly all had boxes within the ground so to a certain extent it was a labour of love.

We made the deadline by the skin of our teeth – I remember the television cameras were covering the Spurs game and the fire officer wasn't going to let them into their area just before kick-off because a door was missing! We had to get a joiner out double quick.

Did I panic? Of course not. I always felt we'd make it. At least if I had a couple of twitches I kept

New look St James's Park

Executive boxes: 69 (11 with outside verandas) – 22 East Stand, 36 Milburn Stand and 11 South West Wing).
MILBURN STAND:
Level One: Harvey's Suite, Thomson Newspapers Suite and United Artists Suite.
Level Two: Centenary Club, Directors Guest Lounge, St. James' Suite, Boardroom Club, Simpson Suite, Vice Presidents Suite, Match Sponsors Lounge.
Level Three: Platinum Club.

Level Four: Rover Suite servicing executive boxes.
EAST STAND: St James' Bar, serving executive boxes

SOUTH WEST WING
Level One: New club shop with 5,000 square feet of retail space.
Level Four: Business Centre.
Level Five: Chairman and Directors Suites.
Level Six: Executive Boxes.
Level Seven: Magpie Room Restaurant sitting 120 people.

them strictly to myself. It's no good the troops seeing the General panicking, is it?

Remember what we were trying to do was not just build a stadium for use on match days but a facility including restaurants, conference rooms, etc, etc, which could be used every day from 8 a.m. until midnight. That's how long St. James's Park is open these days.

However, even these facilities aren't what our supporters will get for the rest of their natural life. If you stand still in business you're dead and Newcastle United is a business. I've worked with Sir John Hall for 21 years, I know his dreams and his aspirations, and we'll always look to expand.

St James's Park timetable

	Start	Finish
North Stand	February 15	August 9, 1993
North East	February 15	August 9, 1993
North West	May 10	November 8, 1993
South Stand	January 10	August 15, 1994
South East	September 5	August 14, 1995
(including South Stand and fitting out package)		
South West	November 21	August 14, 1995

Flying

John Gibson . . .

UNITED'S fans were the rock upon which the Hall revolution was built. They were the best thing – sometimes the only thing – of which the club could be justifiably proud before the team and the stadium rose from years of mediocrity.

Long before the phrase Toon Army was concocted Newcastle United were famed for the hordes of black and white fanatics who poured into St. James's Park, a stadium not fit for the 1966 World Cup finals, and across the Tyne Bridge in pursuit of their favourites.

I should know – I've not only witnessed them from the Press box of every top league ground in England, and many abroad, but I came from their ranks. As a schoolboy I stood excitedly at the old Leazes End marvelling at the likes of Wor Jackie, Bobby Mitchell and big Frank Brennan forging an affinity with my home town club which has never died.

What I can say is that in my living memory success has never quite been sustained as it has in recent times and the hope of greater things to come burns in every Geordie breast.

The Toon Army on the march is a phenomenon of modern day soccer. Around 32,000 season ticket holders, sold out crowds of 36,000-plus for every home match and a waiting list of potential supporters is the envy of virtually every other club in the land.

The new Geordie faithful have marched on European cities like Antwerp and Bilbao, just as their fathers visited Rotterdam, Lisbon, and Budapest back in 1969 when the European Fairs Cup was won. And more Continental sojourns lie ahead. Newcastle United are not just about top-class players and shrewd business acumen but about the people who make the club theirs. The team which supports the team.

the flag

TOON ARMY ON THE MARCH TO GLORY

FAN-TASTIC!

◀ Newcastle and Bilbao fans come together after the UEFA Cup match in Spain.

Freddie Shepherd . . .

OUR fans are remarkable in their devotion, passion – and their cheek! We've tried to build a bridge between the boardroom and the terraces since moving into the club because in the past the decision makers were never accessible to the man in the street.

However, it's produced a few hilarious moments over the years. None more so than when we played at Lucchese in the Anglo Italian Cup. A punter turned up at our hotel with some other fans pleading poverty. It transpired that he had told his lass on the Saturday that he was going out for a pint of milk but instead went to St. James's Park.

Straight after the game he began hitchhiking over to Northern Italy but got mugged on the Paris Metro. He hadn't a penny piece in his pocket!

Being big hearted (or conned!) we told him that by chance there was a spare seat on our plane and he could have it. So he flew home, proud as punch, with the team – an official member of the Newcastle United party. The only trouble was that when we later played at Bari he tried on the same thing. Don't the Geordies push their luck!

Sir John Hall . . .

THE fans are the heart-beat of this football club – it is for them that we strive for success. Indeed my admiration for the Geordies is such that I actually tried to give them the club lock, stock and barrel through a share issue!

Without the support of the fans, both through the turnstiles and through our commercial outlets, we wouldn't be able to compete with the likes of Manchester United. Our turnover has reached £40 million a year and it needs to go even higher.

Yes, we've had to make some harsh decisions along the way which haven't always met with universal approval but that's because there is a price to pay for success. And I'm determined we'll be successful and help regenerate the area.

I'm a decision maker during the week but when it comes to match days I'm a bundle of nerves – many a time I just get up and go behind the scenes for a cup of coffee. The pressure is just too much. I feel so powerless.

I'll turn away and Lady Mae has to tell me "You can look now – the ball is in their half!" I'm just a fan like everyone else.

TOON ARMY ON THE MARCH TO GLORY

FAN-TASTIC!

Douglas Hall . . .

BY any stretch of the imagination this was a sensational transfer – it hit us like a bombshell at first just as it hit not only our fans but the rest of the country as well. Without question the fee – £7 million overall – set the trend for the huge transfers which were to follow.

Funnily enough, at the time Kevin was looking to buy someone to play alongside Coley. We'd put a blockbuster of a bid in for Les Ferdinand but QPR said they'd be lynched if they sold him right there and then. However we'd be first in the queue in the summer, not that I felt it meant much!

KK was also chasing Chris Armstrong but Crystal Palace were messing us about over the fee and Kevin stuck to his guns. He wasn't prepared to enter into an auction.

I was sitting at home when the phone rang. It was Freddie Shepherd, who said he had Kevin Keegan with him and could they come over. I was immediately curious and asked why but Freddie said he couldn't talk on the phone. It was dynamite.

My mind ran riot – did KK want more money to get Armstrong or was it even more serious? Sure enough, in eight minutes flat the front door bell rang and in they came.

KK came out with it straight away. "Would you sell Andy Cole?" he asked me. No, I replied. "Not for £10 million?" Er, not really! By now, I was all at sea but Kevin ploughed on.

He emphasised how much he'd always wanted Keith Gillespie but Manchester United wouldn't sell then added: "Alex Ferguson has been on the phone. He wants Cole and will let me have Gillespie. We've agreed a fee but it's up to you to give your blessing." My head was whirling and I spluttered something about us being lynched.

Quietly, KK explained his reasoning behind the transfer – he valued Gillespie at £2.5 million which made it an £8.5 million deal and stressed that we'd never get the opportunity of another

▲ TAKING THE FLAK – Keegan explains to Newcastle fans why he had sold Coley

Douglas Hall . . .

package like that in our lifetime.

He felt United were a bit too predictable and wanted to change things round. Gillespie and the cash would allow him to do that. I began thinking about the fact that Andy was going through a dry spell as far as goals were concerned and that at the end of the season we were to put him in hospital for an operation on his shin-splints. It didn't seem too outrageous after all.

"But who do we replace him with? was what I wanted to know. 'Leave that to me,' replied Keegan. The next step was how to handle the Press and dad.

Freddie Shepherd . . .

MANCHESTER United were playing at Sheffield United in the FA Cup that night and KK, Freddie Fletcher and myself went down by car. We met John Hall down there and to be fair he was marvellous about the whole thing backing KK's judgment.

On the way down, Kevin broke the news to Andy Cole on the phone. Andy didn't want to leave and made that very clear. However, Keegan persuaded him it was a great opportunity for everyone and he eventually agreed to talk to Man U.

Ferguson pulled Gillespie out of the game that night and we all met afterwards in a Sheffield hotel. Fergie actually acted as Gillespie's agent when we talked personal terms – the whole deal was transacted the way transfer deals should be. Manchester United were first rate.

Around midnight Freddie Fletcher said to Keith: "Were you a member of the boys brigade?" and when they both broke into song about it I knew we had a deal!

We let Man U break the news to the world because the final piece of the jigsaw was their discussions with Andy and his medical. They had to complete the transfer and so it was natural for them to hold a Press conference when they were ready.

It was front page news, of course, and predictably our fans reacted with amazement and then anger – after all, Newcastle United had been a selling club in the old days.

Quite a few punters turned up at St. James's and KK decided to speak to them personally. We all went downstairs and he said his piece. Later John Hall got off a London train at Durham to go to the training ground and talk to supporters. They both showed a lot of bottle but then when you do something like we did the paying customer deserves an explanation.

Kevin Keegan . . .

THIS was a mega, mega deal but it was the right thing at the right time. I didn't feel any other club would offer us the same amount of cash plus a player who could develop like Keith Gillespie. Coley was struggling with us and we were predictable though it wasn't his fault.

I took an awful lot of stick over the transfer which I'll never forget. It was natural to speak to the fans about it – they could only have faith in me if they heard words from my own lips. I also took stick for not replacing Cole quickly but I wasn't prepared to go to the seventh or eighth striker on my shopping list. Filling Andy Cole's boots was going to be hard enough without signing someone I didn't really want.

● GOLDEN BOY – George Weah receives his World Footballer of the Year trophy

WEAH HAVE BEEN CONNED

United protest as £4.2m deal is killed off

18 May, 1995

Terry McDermott...

TO be truthful we were duped over George Weah. We agreed a fee with his club Paris St Germain but they sold him behind our backs to Italian giants AC Milan without letting us talk to the player. Who knows what would have happened had we been able to put our case – aye, even in competition with Milan.

It was obvious that PSG wanted him to go to Italy and used us. That feeling was underlined when Weah came out in the season just ended and said he would have been happy to have talked to us and that Premier League s o c c e r appealed to him.

The quality of the man is unquestioned. Some of our fans mightn't have known too much about him when we went in but he has since been voted World Footballer of the Year.

Douglas Hall...

THE whole thing became a mess. We agreed terms with Paris St Germain by fax and were waiting to go over to France to argue details of the payments and meet Weah. Freddie Shepherd and myself were booked to fly to America on the Monday morning for a meeting with representatives of three ice hockey clubs as part of our Newcastle United Sporting Club plans. However Kevin Keegan phoned to say that he needed us to go over to Paris with him on the Sunday to clinch the Weah transfer.

That was it – we cancelled America and instead booked tickets to Paris with Kevin. Then, out of the blue, he came back a few hours later to say: 'You won't believe it, Weah has signed for AC Milan.'

Now it was back to Plan A for us and at 8 p.m. on the Sunday night we re-booked for New York!

By six o'clock the following morning I was with Freddie at Newcastle Airport – but for some reason the computer wouldn't book our luggage through to New York and we had to pick it up at Heathrow. It was a bit irritating but we collected our bags down there, checked them in again, and headed for the Concorde lounge. It was now 9am and for some reason I got a premonition that something terrible could happen. I fly all over the world yet I felt uneasy, apprehensive. I honestly thought I might die. It was such a strong feeling that I actually phoned my solicitor while we were waiting for the flight to be called and gave him a message to pass on to my wife if anything happened. He tried to re-assure me but I insisted.

When we boarded a party of Buddhist monks suddenly appeared in the aisle in full orange robes clicking the symbols tied to their fingers. It was all unreal.

Anyway, the engines roared and we were off – only something was obviously terribly wrong because the pilot aborted take-off at the end of the runway. The emergency services were called out and came screaming over the tarmac towards us. It was frightening.

We were all hauled off the plane and back in the terminal the message came over that a second plane would be available in an hour.

'To hell with that,' we thought. Enough is enough. We both headed for King's Cross and got the train home. We weren't meant to get George Weah or go to America. But out of it all we signed Les Ferdinand and that wasn't bad, was it?

◀ CHANGE OF TACK – when George Weah signed for AC Milan Newcastle switched their attention to his team-mate David Ginola ▼

WEAH HAVE BEEN CONNED

United protest as £4.2m deal is killed off

18 May, 1995

NEWCASTLE United today accused Paris St Germain of dirty tricks after a £4.2 million bid for superstriker George Weah fell through.

And United are so furious about the conduct of the French club they are ready to protest to UEFA.

◀ READY FOR A FIGHT – Sir John Hall

Sir John Hall . . .

GEORGE WEAH'S London-based agent first alerted us about the player's availability. Kevin knew how good he was and we faxed off an offer of £4.2 million. We received a fax back accepting our bid and Kevin, Douglas and Freddie arranged to fly to Paris.

PSG wouldn't let us talk to Weah before their game with Cannes, which was fair enough, but everything was set. Then out of the blue the agent rang back to say Weah was going to AC Milan and everything was off.

Paris St Germain didn't even have the courtesy to inform us direct. We even had to send THREE faxes to Paris before they confirmed that the deal was off.

It transpired that AC had originally offered £3 million and we were obviously used to jack up the price to £5 million which is what PSG eventually got.

It wasn't an honourable thing to do and we put everything in the hands of our lawyers.

We were prepared to go all the way, which would have meant a civil case with UEFA regulations not covering such actions, but when Kevin wanted to sign David Ginola from Paris St Germain shortly afterwards we closed the book on Weah.

◀ WAITING GAME –
United had to wait
for a new financial
year at Wimbledon
before defender
Warren Barton put
pen to paper and
signed for the
Magpies.

KK SNAPS UP £4M BARTON

5 June, 1995

Freddie Shepherd . . .

WARREN BARTON became our club record buy at £4 million for a couple of days until we unveiled Les Ferdinand at £6 million. In fact we'd shaken hands with Warren a long time before the deal became official but it was put on ice for tax reasons!

Let me explain – Wimbledon are a small club which lives by selling its top players for big money. Think of Dave Beasant, Andy Thorn, Dennis Wise, Vinnie Jones, Keith Curle, John Scales, and John Fashanu. Quite a list, isn't it? They try to sell one a year and didn't want Barton to go until the following financial year. So we had to sit tight safe in the knowledge that he would be our player.

Douglas Hall . . .

WE'D had a good offer from Glasgow Celtic for Marc Hottiger and KK wanted to bring in Barton for his versatility – he could play in other positions as well as right-back. As it happened the Celtic deal fell through and Hottiger didn't move

to Everton until some time later.

Freddie Shepherd . . .

KEVIN KEEGAN and Freddie Fletcher had driven down to London to complete the £4 million transfer and were going direct to Goodison Park afterwards for our match with Everton. When they got near the ground they hit a huge traffic jam.

Time was getting on and Kevin became agitated. Suddenly he leapt out of the passenger seat and legged it up to Goodison leaving a bemused Freddie Fletch stuck in a line of bumper-to-bumper traffic and the car door open! It's always exciting when we hit the transfer trail.

WORTH EVERY PENNY

Keegan's verdict on United's £6m new boy Ferdie

June 7, 1995

Freddie Fletcher . . .

SOME transfers are completed in a flash, this one took 18 months. We almost got Les twice before it was finally done and dusted. I seemed to spend most of my time contacting Richard Thompson at QPR lodging Ferdinand bids.

We started off wanting him to play alongside Andy Cole and ended up getting him as Cole's replacement. First, the fans turned against QPR, which put the mockers on a £5 million deal, and then the next year we almost got him before the transfer deadline but they were in relegation trouble and didn't want to sell until they were safe.

As soon as the season was over Rangers were anxious to cash in while Ferdie was still under contract. We had a £5.5 million offer on the table but Aston Villa upped the price to £6 million and were given permission to talk to him. It was now clear cut – we either matched Villa or forgot about it.

There was no way QPR would accept £5.5 million with £6 million already lodged. In we went again and Les was hidden away in an hotel south of Wynyard to meet KK.

Kevin Keegan . . .

I ALWAYS held up Les as the complete centre-forward – and the passing of time wasn't going to change that. Besides, he kept doing well against us to remind me of his qualities.

I remember one day early on climbing into my car at St. James's Park to go and watch Ferdinand play for QPR at Liverpool. Andy Cole just happened to be going in to collect his mail and I yelled: "Andy, what are you doing tonight?" Before he knew what was happening he was sitting next to me on his way to Merseyside! Cole was scoring an awful lot of goals

for us but I told him I wanted him just to watch Les play – no one else.

To see how he led his line, his appreciation of players around him and his team work. I felt that Andy, a young player, could learn from that.

At the time I wanted Ferdinand to play alongside Cole but in the end he was the striker I brought in to take over Andy's mantle. Sometimes perserverence is the name of the game.

◀ Soccer legend Pele hands over the PFA Player of the Year trophy for 1995-96 to Les Ferdinand

Terry McDermott . . .

BY the time we finally nailed Les I was out of the country on my summer holidays. It's ironic how things sometimes work out!

We'd been in for him for so long and obviously I knew everything that was happening but I was due to go to Minorca with the family for a spot of sun and the deal still wasn't done by the time the McDermotts hit the skies.

It was supposed to be a time to relax and recharge the batteries for the new season but I couldn't. I knew what Les meant to our plans and I was on edge – there's many a last minute slip-up when completing transfers. So in

between putting on the sun cream and entertaining the kids I was trying – discreetly – to find out what was happening back home.

It went on for days until finally there I was sitting in front of the telly watching Sky News. Before the break for adverts it said "coming up next, sport." I was half interested, of course, but suddenly my telly screen was filled with a picture of Ferdinand on the St. James's Park pitch with the announcement of a record £6 million signing. I almost fell of my chair with relief.

I guess our fans knew as quickly as the assistant manager that Newcastle United had signed Les!

Juventus were asking £8.5 million and
Baggio wanted £64,000 per week.

UNITED GO FOR BAGGIO

23 July, 1995

Douglas Hall . . .

WE'D just smashed the club record transfer fee twice in a matter of days for Warren Barton and Les Ferdinand but we've never been a club without ambition. I love the cut-and-thrust of deals and for a bit of fun I had a black-and-white shirt made up with Roberto Baggio's name on the back.

It was lying on the back seat of my car on the day of the Ferdinand Press conference at St. James's Park and, of course, the fans spotted it. Soon, even the TV cameras were taking shots of the shirt, not knowing whether to believe it or not.

Actually, it wasn't a gimmick. We made a genuine effort to sign Baggio, rated the best player in the world – I honestly thought we'd get him.

Freddie Shepherd . . .

I SENT a fax off to Juventus asking about Baggio's availability and got one back stating that we had no chance.

They talked about being a club which built empires not lost them.

I still have the fax framed at home.

However, we wouldn't take no for an answer and, like the great explorers we are, we got on a plane, flew to Italy, and knocked on their door.

Douglas Hall . . .

WHEN we got to Turin there was no one at the ground to see us. We were exasperated because we knew the fee Juventus were seeking and it wasn't out of our range. Our money is as good as anyone else's so why couldn't we enter into talks?

Freddie Shepherd, Freddie Fletcher and Terry MacDermott were with me and we'd also taken a local Italian restaurateur, Franco, with us as interpreter – Kevin Keegan was on holiday. We spoke to an agent in England telling him of our problems and he agreed to fly out to set up a meeting with Italy's No.1 agent – a guy who had all the clout in their transfer dealings. We were to meet Mr Big the following day in Juventus's restaurant.

The meeting was scheduled for 12 noon but by one o'clock he still hadn't arrived. The food was all set out on the table but we were sick at being messed around and got up and left. We went back to our hotel and packed – the rest of the party were flying back to Newcastle but I was going to Marbella to meet the family who were on holiday.

I had a later flight and the rest of our party had already left. I was sitting in reception waiting to go when in walked the Italian agent who'd kept us waiting. "Let's go back to the restaurant," he pleaded. He told me Juventus were asking £8.5 million and that Baggio wanted £64,000 per week. 'No way', I replied. 'That's bloody ridiculous.' However he insisted that AC Milan were willing to give Roberto £3.2 million a year.

It was the start of the Italian transfer week – the one week in the season when clubs can do deals – and he suggested we went to this hotel in Milan which is known as the marketplace where agents and clubs all meet in different rooms to thrash out business. He would speak with Baggio.

We drove to Milan and this Italian agent took me to a trotting track outside the San Siro Stadium where all he seemed interested in was gambling. I got well sick, shot off back to my hotel, and arranged to fly on to Marbella the next day. Even then I received a phone call in Spain asking if they could bring Baggio to see me. The deal seemed to be off then on but it went dead again and the next thing I knew Baggio had signed for Milan.

OOH AAH GEORDIE GINOLA

7 July, 1995

Freddie Shepherd . . .

THIS was probably our easiest and smoothest transfer deal from abroad. As in the case of most of Kevin's signings he'd had his eye on Ginola for a while and a few days after we pulled out of the John Salako deal on medical grounds he told us he could get him.

We'd had a bit of trouble with David's club Paris St. Germain over George Weah but we faxed them our bid and they accepted it. Honest, at £2.5 million Ginola has turned out to be the steal of the decade.

Anyway, David, his wife and agent flew over from Paris and we met them in a suite at the Gosforth Park Hotel – Russell Jones, Freddie Fletcher, Terry Mac and I were in our party. And what was really surprising is that Ginola didn't want to be part of the financial talks on his contract. In fact, he didn't even want to be there during the discussions!

We knew Arsenal had been dabbling for him and he had just been up to Glasgow Celtic but his wife didn't fancy that particular move too much. So it was important to make a good impression

not just in terms of the club but the area.

David and his missus wanted to look round Tyneside and take in the MetroCentre while we discussed cash with his agent Dominique Rocheteau so we pulled off a little stroke to make things easier.

David could speak decent enough English but his wife wasn't really fluent so we got in touch with Jim O'Connor, the director of our catering division, who spoke fluent French and got him to take the Ginolas on their sight-seeing tour. They looked like a couple of glamorous film stars and we treated them appropriately.

It took two or three hours to thrash out the financial deal but we sensed that David was a special player and we went that extra mile to get him. His presence was immediate.

When David came back all he wanted to know was whether we could get him a housekeeper, gardener and whatever because he had them in his home in Paris.

Sir John Hall . . .

AFTER the Press conference the following day I took David and his charming wife Coraline into the Strawberry pub round the back of the ground to meet the fans.

When we walked in the people sitting there almost fell off their seats – the young girls were taken with David and the fellas couldn't stop eyeing Coraline. I guess that's when David first got his taste for Newcastle Brown Ale.

Terry McDermott . . .

TERMS were actually agreed with Paris St Germain on a caravan site in Amble – honest! Kevin Keegan was in America and I was having a day out with the family and friends when my mobile phone rang. It was the president of Ginola's club trying to fix a fee and we haggled away. He could speak broken English and had a lady interpretor with him for the difficult parts. It wasn't easy under the circumstances but when David came to the North East it was. All he wanted to do was sign.

Kevin Keegan . . .

THIS was the last candle on the cake that close season but I honestly didn't see it as a major signing at the price. Medical opinion was that Scott Sellars might not come back from a serious injury so I wanted a left-sided player and Ginola was tailor-made for us.

I've never ever seen a player like him. I believe Newcastle fans want to be entertained. They would rather see a magnificent draw than a 1-0 win ground out through defensive tactics. And David was ideal for the way I like to play.

◀ GLOVE BROTHERS – Shaka signed for Kevin Keegan then made a dash to Edinburgh to meet his new team-mates.

SHAKE ON IT SHAKA

£1.75m Hislop 'yes' to United

9 August, 1995

Freddie Shepherd. . .

TRANSFERS can take time for a lot of reasons – availability of the player, agreeing a fee, personal terms, moving the family up to the North East. Well, this one was different. The problem here was that Shaka's club Reading had to give him a huge slice of the transfer fee.

They had signed him from American soccer and inserted a clause in his contract guaranteeing him a big percentage of any monies received if he moved on. It proved to be a real stumbling block because Reading were to get nothing like the £1.75 million we had offered. It wasn't our problem, of course, but nevertheless it didn't help us wrap up a quick deal. In the end Shaka dropped a lot of cash because of his ambition to play Premier League football with a big club.

He signed for us in the afternoon at St.

James's Park and then asked: "Where are you going now?" I explained that we were playing a pre-season match in Edinburgh that night and he shocked us by asking: "Can I come?"

He and his wife hadn't even booked into an hotel and here he was wanting to jump into a car and motor another hundred or so miles over the border. Anyway, I drove Shaka and Desha up to the game with Hearts – it was a testimonial match for our old player John Robertson – and after the game I took him downstairs where Kevin Keegan introduced him to his new teammates. It was the early hours of the next morning before I finally got him to the Gosforth Park Hotel to book in!

◀ DOUBLE TOPS – England rugby star Rob Andrew joined Kevin Keegan at the Newcastle Sporting Club revolution

Newcastle swoop to land England star Andrew – "the Keegan of rugby"

ROBSMACKED

21 September, 1995

Freddie Shepherd . . .

THE concept of a Newcastle United Sporting Club belonged to Sir John who had seen what Sporting Lisbon and the Spanish giants Real Madrid and Barcelona had achieved on the back of their football clubs. He felt that, while soccer would always be the flagship, there was no reason why the Geordies shouldn't benefit from top class sport across the board.

As a result, we now own Newcastle Gosforth Rugby Union club, the Wasps ice hockey team, the Comets basketball side, a boxing club under former world champion Glenn McCrory, and take part in motor racing with the Lister Storm outfit.

However I suppose our move into Rugby Union shortly after it became professional is what really caught the headlines especially when we swooped to sign England star Rob Andrew as our player-manager. In rugby terms that was as mind-boggling as the day we got Kevin Keegan.

The move for Gosforth was as breathtaking in terms of speed as our bid for Andrew. We met their committee after an informal approach from them and Douglas Hall insisted on an answer to our proposals within 48 hours. Frankly, I never thought they would agree that quickly but they did. Next came the appointment of a figurehead. We decided to follow our successful formula with the football club and that meant a charismatic figure with a high profile. One man stood out: Rob Andrew.

But how to get him, that was the problem. We decided the best policy was to take the bull by the horns. We knew the firm he worked for in London so I rang them and asked to be put through to Rob. He came on the line immediately. He didn't know me from Adam but I outlined our position and asked for a meeting. No messing. "We better consult our diaries then," said Andrew. "No, let's meet tonight," I insisted. "We can get down to Lon-

don." He was honestly flabbergasted. "I admire your speed," he said. "Okay then, tonight."

We met at Shepherds Restaurant – and no, I don't own it unfortunately! We booked a private room in the back which we'd used on several occasions for other Newcastle United business. We knew Martin the maitre d'hotel was discreet and would keep everything confidential. Douglas Hall, Rob and myself were the only ones present and we cracked open a couple of bottles of Chilean wine with the meal. Within hours we'd changed Rob Andrew's life – he'd arrived with a shining black eye sustained playing rugby and we hit him right between the eyes!

But he came back fighting. He asked for the weekend to sit down with his financial adviser and by the time he arrived in Newcastle on the Monday Rob had a business plan to put before us on how he saw the rugby club going. That was impressive. We knew Andrew had the presence of a Keegan and that international players would follow him into the club. And that's what happened.

Douglas Hall . . .

IRONICALLY just before we moved into Rugby Union we'd agreed a deal to form a Rugby League club. Our operations manager Paul Stevens knew the Rugby League chief executive Maurice Lindsay from his days at Gateshead Council and Maurice came up to see us in Newcastle. He was really enthusiastic but, frankly, time was against us putting a side together in time to join the Super League. However, it was made clear that we would be welcome in 1997 and, despite what people might think with us going into Rugby Union, we are still looking seriously at a RL participation.

◀ MARATHON
DEAL – £7.5m Tino
Asprilla signed for
Newcastle after one
of the most
complicated
transfer deals
handled by the St
James's Park club

THE DEAL'S DONE
Aspro joins Magpies for £7.5m

7 February, 1996

Douglas Hall . . .

WE actually went for Asprilla and Boksic simultaneously – not many people know that as they say! Speculation was rife when we flew to both Milan and Rome but no one knew for certain what was on because we wouldn't say a word.

With two possible deals running at the same time, and the Italians being cagey in the extreme, the whole thing was rather complicated so let's go through it kick-by-kick.

KK had fancied Asprilla for a long, long time before we embarked on our final moves. Kevin, Freddie Shepherd and myself flew over to Italy to try and open negotiations with the idea of flying on to Sweden in an effort to get Jesper Blomqvist as well though that idea quickly fell through. The first part of the Asprilla saga was relatively painless – we booked into the Hotel D'umo in Milan and met with the Parma chief executive and his son. Terms of £7.5 million were agreed subject to Faustino's medical and personal terms.

His agent was in South America so we arranged to meet him later in London. When we were entering into talks Kevin heard that Alen Boksic at Lazio might also be available so we decided to keep our options open in case Asprilla's terms were horrendous. Sure enough, things got a bit complicated and it began to look as though Boksic would be a bit cheaper.

The next move was to fly out to Rome to meet the Lazio owner and Boksic – only when we booked into our hotel we found that the Welsh international squad who were playing Italy were also staying there and the place was swarming with journalists! Freddie Shep introduced me to Ian Rush saying: 'Here's your chain-smoking lookalike' – it was a bit of light relief as we were dodging and weaving.

We got messed about by Lazio so we went down to lunch for a break and discussed whether we should buy both Boksic AND Asprilla. KK quite fancied it but Terry Mac, who had joined us on this trip, felt we just needed one forward.

We actually ended up doing a deal with Cragnotti, their owner, only for Boksic to get a bit greedy with Lazio so we decided to fly up to Milan on the private plane to talk to Asprilla and Parma. There was some difficulty over personal terms but the day after we got home Parma phoned up to say Tino had accepted them. Another hurdle overcome.

■ BOKSIC

NEWCASTLE United have wrapped up the marathon £7.5m transfer negotiations for Colombian hit-man Faustino Asprilla.

By JOHN GIBSON

And all that's left to officially bring two weeks of on-off talks to a successful conclusion is the granting of a work permit.

THE DEAL'S DONE

Aspro joins Magpies for £7.5m

Freddie Shepherd...

WHILE we kept silent Parma were spouting about Asprilla which meant the photographers were door-stepping Newcastle Airport ready for his arrival but we flew him into Teesside instead and took him to Wynyard Hall where he had dinner with Sir John and Lady Mae, Douglas Hall, fellow director Russell Jones and myself. The next morning we whisked him up to St. James's Park and he went off for his medical.

That took longer and longer until we heard from the medical people that they wanted more scans over a possible knee injury. When you're paying £7.5 million you're extra cautious – the problems were: when had it happened and what was the rate of deterioration? We couldn't sign Asprilla anyway because we had to apply for a work permit and the player must be out of the country while the DoE consider your request, so he flew back out to Parma.

Douglas Hall...

FREDDIE Shep, Russell Jones, Freddie Fletcher and I were due to fly to Daytona Beach in Florida to see our car, the Lister Storm, compete in the famous 24-hour race and we decided to go via Concorde.

We flew to Paris to pick up Concorde bound for New York when we heard that Parma were kicking up a stink over Tino's medical. So we despatched Russell and Freddie Fletch over to Italy instead and we caught Concorde to America.

Phone calls were flying across the Atlantic from Italy and Newcastle but they saw Tino's medical records and everything was sorted out with Parma's lawyers.

One of our most complicated deals ever was finally completed with handshakes all round.

Kevin Keegan . . .

I WANTED Asprilla because I knew he was a world class player and all the rubbish about his past off the park never bothered me a bit. Some of it was scandalous but I never wavered in going for him because I always make up my own mind and I received top class backing from the board in my endeavours – the only reason for the hold-up was medical. Nothing else.

I saw Tino play for Colombia against England at Wembley and was struck by his enthusiasm and workrate as well as his obvious ability. Tino wanted to play for us and I wanted him. End of story.

Freddie Shepherd . . .

THERE is always a laugh, even in a complicated, controversial deal like this one. And it came when we sent Freddie Fletcher and Russell Jones over to Italy as our peacemakers after Parma accused us of trying to use Tino's injury as an excuse to pull out of the transfer. At the end of the tricky talks the Parma president said a few words in Italian and our lads replied: "Thank you very much" shaking his hand in turn. A bemused interpretor asked: "Why do you shake hands? He's just called you little s***s."

Freddie Shepherd . . .

WE'D learned our lesson with John Salako and Tino Asprilla – no more deals done in the public glare. Especially when it came to the medical. So we hit the road down to Manchester to meet David Batty in secret.

We were not only going to talk terms with him and his agent but to do the medical out of town too. That way, if anything went wrong we could shake hands, come home, and say nothing. It made sense for the sake of the player as well as ourselves.

I motored down with general manager Russell Cushing and our physio Derek Wright and we met in a hotel just outside Manchester United's ground. Ironic, I suppose, as they were our big rivals in the championship race.

Just as David Ginola had done David opted out of the talks on his personal deal. His agent talked cash with me while Derek Wright took David to a nearby private hospital for his medical. Batty asked for a little time to mull over the transfer and we arranged to meet him on the Saturday lunchtime before our match with Manchester City at Maine Road.

Unfortunately, City couldn't provide us with a private room and we had to meet in their public restaurant on the ground. We managed to find a table tucked away in the corner and thrashed out a couple of small points. His medical was okay, thank goodness, and a handshake meant Batty was our player. I had been expecting to meet a Yorkshire terrier but instead I found him a pussycat! Sure, David can look after himself on the park but off it he's a smashing little fella.

Batty sat behind us during the match and decided to leave just before the end to make certain he got away from the ground without the Press nailing him. We were losing 3-2 when he left and no doubt he was well pleased afterwards to learn we'd drawn 3-3.

I guess what made this transfer different to our others is that we gave him a secret medical and actually finalised the deal on another Premier League ground.

GOTCHA!

KEV GETS HIS MAN AS BATTY SIGNS

29 February, 1996

Terry McDermott . . .

WE were interested in David Batty for an awful long time before we eventually got him – indeed, the deal was on ice at one time for a whole month. And take no notice of all the talk that we paid £4 million. We didn't – the fee was £3.5 million. In fact that's what the hold-up was all about. Blackburn Rovers wanted £4 million and Kevin Keegan wasn't prepared to pay it.

The point with Blackburn is that all deals – in and out – must eventually go through Jack Walker and he doesn't live on the mainland which causes some difficulty. David told us afterwards that he'd tried to get a meeting with him to thrash things out but hadn't been able to arrange it. I don't think Jack Walker wanted to sell Batty and I can understand why. There are also complications sometimes with the way transfer fees are paid – the period of time covered by the instalments, etc.

I spent five or six hours with him on the day he came up here and all he could talk about was how happy he was that the waiting was at an end. That's how desperate he was to sign and such an attitude is important when you take a player be he a kid or a superstar. He needs to want to play for you.

A lot of fans saw Batty as merely a ball winner – a little tough guy – but I honestly think that his passing is the best part of his game. Perhaps that's now dawned on a few folk.

◀ THUMBS UP – Kevin Keegan salutes the fans after the last game of the 1995-96 season at St James's Park had confirmed United as Premier League runners-up

Defiant United take it on the chin and vow: this is just the start

BLOODIED BUT UNBOWED

May 6, 1996

Sir John Hall . . .

NEWCASTLE UNITED finished the 1995-96 season in their best league position since 1927 and that, whatever disappointments we might have experienced along the way, is an achievement in itself. We are now on Concorde instead of flying Dakota and we're ready for lift-off. The future is ours.

We've come an awful long way in a short space of time – we're ahead of schedule and that's what counts. We've tackled every obstacle and achieved our objectives – we've brought St. James's Park in line with the Taylor Report, we've structured our management team and we've built a squad of players capable of taking us to the top of the Pre-

mier League. And we've done it a year ahead of what I planned.

Now we can spread ourselves even farther in the pursuit of perfection, taking in our soccer academy for the Geordie kids and our sports medicine and science programme for the treatment of players. We've already spread into schools and the community to promote the gospel according to Newcastle United.

What I've witnessed since moving into the boardroom has convinced me that we are on the verge of great things. We're ambitious and will remain so.

But the road has been a hard and demanding one. There were two battles to be won – first for

▶ WONDER GOAL – Steve Watson scores the Coca-Cola Cup winner for United at Liverpool in one of the top performances of the season

◄ PRAYING
FOR
SUCCESS –
the young fan
and her
Champion
mascot

◀ JOY BEFORE DESPAIR – David Batty is congratulated after scoring against his old club Blackburn at Ewood Park – but two late goals killed a championship dream

Sir John Hall . . .

Defiant United take it on the chin and vow: this is just the start

BLOODIED BUT UNBOWED

control of the club and then to make the club successful. The shares war was long and demanding and, once we made it, I was fully aware that was only the beginning. After such a public fight we had to deliver – and in a spectacular way. Yet nothing prepared me for what was ahead.

I had been a very successful businessman but I didn't realise how much football takes over your life. How much it eats into your private life until it almost doesn't exist. This is without doubt the most physically and mentally exhausting job I've ever had.

It's the emotional aspect of football which is so stressful. If a fan buys a ticket he believes he's bought 100 per cent of you. You have a public responsibility you never have in the same way in private business. Anything up to 250,000 Geordies examine and dissect every single decision you make – that is life in the fast lane.

We have supporters all over the world. My diary at the end of the season included trips to Dublin and Iceland to talk to some of those far-flung fans. They all want part of the black and whites.

But it is something I accept. It is

the price you pay to make Newcastle United great again. And we will be. We are so close already and we've just begun.

In the season just ended we set the pace for so long. We went out in front almost from the first hurdle and in the Grand National that's the hardest way to ride the course. In the end we were caught in the home straight but the point is we've narrowed the gap between us and Manchester United on the field. They are now within our sights.

Kevin Keegan has been impatient for some silverware and we can all understand that – we all feel the same way. Now, however, we're in a genuine position to strike out for that. We might have made a rod for our own backs by finishing second and looking for even more improvement but we're not afraid.

When you saw our fans distraught and in tears at Liverpool and Blackburn Rovers you know what the club means to them. And to see those same supporters stand in the ground for an hour after the last game of the season to hail Kevin and the players was a heartwarming moment I'll never forget. They are the people we work for and the reason why, having hopefully given them back so much of their pride, we intend to take them all the way.

▶ AGONY – David Ginola

Acknowledgements

My sincere thanks for the total co-operation given by Newcastle United's directors and management team in the compiling of this book. They gave their valuable time unstintingly.

Thanks, too, to my Evening Chronicle colleague John Stokoe for the design and production of the book – a mammoth task carried out with true black and white dedication – and to Chronicle cartoonist Geoff Laws.

The splendid colour photographs were provided in the main by the Chronicle picture library and by United photographer Ian Horricks.

Several other people gave of their time with cover design, proof reading and scouring our library for the appropriate headlines. It was indeed a team effort.

JOHN GIBSON

If you would like to purchase any of the photographs in this book simply telephone the Evening Chronicle Photosales Department on 0191 2016001 to request on order form.

Unfortunately, we can only supply photographs which have been taken by our own photographers.